I0697959

UNCOVERING THE UNIVERSE OF FUNDAMENTAL CLASSIFIED ASSOCIATIONS (VPNS): INVESTIGATING THE MODERNIZED SPACE SAFELY AND SUBTLY

2

Contents

In the present interconnected world, where modernized correspondences structure a fundamental piece of our everyday schedules, ensuring the security and assurance of online activities has become chief. People and organizations the same have looked for powerful methods for shielding their web-based presence because of the ascent in digital dangers, information breaks, and security concerns. Enter the Virtual Secret Association, or VPN, a fundamental resource planned to make a strong and classified relationship over the web.

1.2 Why should you use a VPN?

The decision to use a VPN begins from various factors, each adding to the creating reputation of these organizations:

Security Affirmation:
With the rising stress over electronic security, individuals go to VPNs to protect their web practices from perception, whether by government substances, Web access Providers (ISPs), or noxious performers.

Security Improvement:
VPNs scramble data, making it out and out more earnestly for developers and cybercriminals to catch and exploit sensitive information. This ends up being particularly basic while using public Wi-Fi associations, which are helpless against security breaks.

2. Picking a VPN Provider

As the interest for VPN organizations continues to rise, a lot of providers have emerged, each offering noteworthy components and limits. Picking the right VPN provider is a fundamental decision that requires mindful idea.

2.1 Investigating VPN Providers:
Lead comprehensive investigation on potential VPN providers, considering factors, for instance, reputation, client studies, and the provider's situation on client assurance.

2.2 Things to Contemplate:
Survey key components, for instance, server regions, affiliation speed, logging methodologies, and client care. A strong VPN provider should offer a concordance between

generous security components and simple to utilize handiness.

2.3 Notable VPN Organizations:
Examine unquestionably the most renowned VPN organizations keeping watch, each with its resources and weaknesses. Consider providers like NordVPN, ExpressVPN, and CyberGhost, among others, and difference their commitments with line up with your specific necessities.

In the going with sections of this helper, we will plunge further into the valuable pieces of getting involved with a VPN organization, downloading and presenting VPN programming, planning the VPN client, and effectively utilizing a VPN to ensure a strong and private online understanding. Whether you're a fledgling or a refined client, this exhaustive helper intends to empower you with the data and capacities critical to investigate the universe of VPNs successfully.

2. Picking a VPN Supplier

Choosing the right VPN supplier is a basic move toward guaranteeing a safe and solid virtual confidential organization experience. With a heap of choices accessible, clients need to weigh different variables to find a supplier that lines up with their particular necessities and needs.

2.1 Exploring VPN Suppliers

Prior to focusing on a VPN supplier, it is fundamental for lead exhaustive examination. Think about the accompanying viewpoints:

Notoriety and Audits:
Really look at the standing of potential VPN suppliers through internet based audits, discussions, and suggestions. Respectable suppliers are probably going to have positive surveys and a background marked by conveying solid administrations.

Privacy Statements:
Look at the supplier's security strategy to comprehend how they handle client information. If the service provider does not store any information about your online activities, look for a strict no-logs policy.

Jurisdiction:
Think about the lawful ward of the VPN supplier. Users' privacy may be compromised by jurisdictions that

have data retention laws or are members of international surveillance alliances.

Security Elements:
Assess the security highlights presented by every supplier. Search for conventions like OpenVPN or IKEv2, solid encryption norms (AES-256), and extra elements, for example, an off button for added security.

Concurrent Associations:
Check the quantity of synchronous associations permitted by the VPN supplier.

2.2 Elements to Consider

Server Areas:
The number and appropriation of server areas can influence your internet based insight. Suppliers with a worldwide server network

offer more choices for getting to content and better execution.

Rate of Connection:
VPN administrations can influence web speed. Search for suppliers that focus on high velocity associations, particularly assuming you participate in exercises like streaming or web based gaming.

Gadget Similarity:
Guarantee that the VPN supplier upholds the gadgets and working frameworks you use. Whether it's Windows, macOS, Android, iOS, or Linux, similarity is vital for a consistent encounter.

2.3 Famous VPN Administrations

Investigate a portion of the main VPN administrations that reliably get positive criticism from clients:

NordVPN:

Known for major areas of strength for its highlights, an immense server organization, and easy to use interface, NordVPN is a famous decision for the two fledglings and high level clients.

ExpressVPN:

ExpressVPN stands apart for its quick and solid associations, easy to understand interface, and an expansive scope of server areas. It likewise has gained notoriety for focusing on client protection.

CyberGhost:

With an accentuation on easy to use plan, CyberGhost offers a huge server organization, hearty security includes, and committed streaming servers for getting to geo-limited content.

Access to the private internet (PIA): PIA is famous for its, areas of strength for reasonableness to protection, and adaptable security settings, making it a number one among protection cognizant clients.

End

Picking a VPN supplier requires cautious thought of your particular necessities and needs. By directing careful exploration, assessing fundamental factors, and investigating famous choices, you can find a VPN administration that lines up with your inclinations, giving a protected and solid internet based insight. The next sections of this guide will discuss the practical aspects of setting up the VPN client and signing up for a VPN service.

3. Getting involved with a VPN Organization

At the point when you've gotten a VPN provider that lines with your prerequisites, the ensuing stage is to get involved with their organization. This incorporates making a record, picking an enrollment plan, and completing the portion cycle.

3.1 Making a Record

Most VPN providers anticipate that clients should create a record before they can start using the assistance. As a rule, follow these means:

Go to the Site of the Supplier:

Go to the power site of the VPN provider you've picked.
Sign up or log in:

Find the "Sign-Up," "Register," or "Create Account" buttons.
Give the crucial information, including a real email address and a strong mystery key.
Verification:

A couple of providers could require email affirmation. Scan your email for a really take a look at interface and comply with the rules.
Account Dashboard:

After affirmation, you may be composed to your record dashboard. Track your login data.

3.2 Picking a Participation Plan

VPN providers regularly offer different enrollment plans,

changing in length and components. Consider your prerequisites and spending plan while picking a course of action:

Participation Plans:

Month to month, yearly, and, surprisingly, longer-term plans are habitually presented by suppliers. Yearly plans are commonly more reasonable than month to month ones.
Components and Cutoff points:

Analyze the highlights that are remembered for each arrangement, for example, the quantity of associations that can be made at the same time.
Consider any cutoff points on information transmission or server access.

Free Starters and Genuine commitments:

A couple of providers offer free starters or unrestricted commitments. Make use of these options to test the assistance before committing.

3.3 Portion Decisions

At the point when you've picked an enrollment plan, this present time is the perfect open door to complete the portion cycle. The majority of VPN providers provide a variety of payment options, including:

Cards accepted for payment:

Most providers recognize critical credit and really look at cards. Safely enter your card details.
PayPal:

PayPal is a well known technique for installment. If security is a concern, using PayPal can add an extra layer of anonymity.
Cryptocurrencies:

A few suppliers acknowledge digital currencies like Bitcoin for further developed security. Your payment is kept even more secret by making this choice.

Other Portion Procedures:

Dependent upon the provider, there may be other portion decisions available, for instance, bank moves or gift vouchers.
End The process of signing up for a VPN service entails making a record, selecting a reasonable membership plan, and finishing the payment. Make sure the arrangement you choose meets

your needs, and take advantage of any opportunities for testing or unconditional guarantees to evaluate the help's presentation. The resulting region of this guide will guide you through downloading and presenting the VPN programming, planning the VPN client, and further developing your VPN experience.

4. Downloading and Presenting VPN Programming

Resulting to getting involved with a VPN organization, the accompanying basic step is to download and present the VPN client programming on your contraption. This cooperation could move possibly depending upon your picked provider and the contraption's functioning system.

4.1 Viable Devices and Operating

Systems Before proceeding, verify that your device and operating system are compatible with the VPN software. Most VPN providers offer clients for different contraptions, including:

Windows: Suitable with structures like Windows 7, 8, and 10.

MacOS: Expected for MacBook, iMac, and other Macintosh contraptions.

Android: acceptable for tablets and smartphones.

iOS: made particularly for iPads and iPhones.

Linux: As often as possible maintained with manual arrangement or dedicated clients.

4.2 Downloading the VPN Client

To download the VPN Client, adhere to these overall directions:

Sign in to your record:

Visit the VPN provider's site and sign in to your record.
Segment for Downloads:

See as the "Download" region on the website. This is commonly obviously shown.
Choose Your Device:

Pick the variation of the VPN client that thinks about to your device and working structure. Providers regularly therefore distinguish your device type.
Begin the Download:

Click on the download association or button to begin the download cooperation.

4.3 Presenting the VPN Client

At the point when the VPN client is downloaded, go on with the foundation:

For Windows and MacOS:
Run the Installer:

Find the downloaded plan record and run the installer.
Follow Foundation Wizard:

Comply with the on-screen rules given by the foundation wizard.
Select an area for establishment, acknowledge the terms, and snap "Introduce."
Ship off the VPN Client:

After foundation is done, ship off the VPN client.
For Phones (Android and iOS):
Android Market or Google Play:

Search for the VPN Application:

Search for the VPN application by making the provider's name in the chase bar.
Introduce and Install:

Subsequent to tapping the application, select "Introduce" or "Download" for Android or iOS.
Start the VPN Software:

Once presented, open the VPN application on your cell.
End

Downloading and presenting the VPN client is an essential push toward spreading out a protected and private affiliation. Persistently download the item from the power website of your picked provider to ensure believability. In the accompanying fragments of this helper, we will cover the arrangement of the VPN client, recalling logging for to your record, picking a server region, and researching additional settings for ideal execution and security.

5. Configuring the VPN Client

Now that you have downloaded and installed the VPN Client, it is time to customize it to meet your specific needs. Signing into your VPN account, selecting a server location, and altering additional settings if necessary are all part of the design cycle.

5.1 Marking In to Your VPN Record

Ship off the VPN Client:

Open the VPN client on your device.
Enter Login Certifications:

Give your username and secret expression, which you made during the record enlistment process.
Remember Me Decision:

For comfort, a few clients offer the "Recall Me" or "Remain Signed In" choices. Use this part considering your security tendencies.
Login:

To get to your VPN record, tap or snap the "Login" button.

5.2 Picking a Server Region

Picking a fitting server region is urgent for improving your VPN experience. Follow this technique:

Server Summary:

The majority of VPN clients display a list of available server locations. This can as often as possible be found on the essential screen.
Select a Server:

Pick a server in light of your prerequisites. Choose a server in a location that meets your needs for safety and protection. For getting to locale bound content, select a server in the best region.
Quick Interface:

The "Speedy Interface" option on some VPN clients directs you to the best server that anyone could hope to find based on your location and preferences.

5.3 Designing Additional Settings

(If Necessary) Depending on your VPN provider and client, you may be able to design additional settings for improved execution and security:

Show Decision:

Pick the VPN show that suits your necessities. OpenVPN, IKEv2, and L2TP/IPsec are typical choices. Because of its wellbeing, OpenVPN is much of the time suggested.

Off button:

Include the off button if it is available. This ensures that expecting the VPN affiliation exits

the blue, all that web traffic is finished to hinder data spills.
Arrangement of the DNS:

A couple of clients license you to plan DNS settings. Using the VPN provider's DNS servers can redesign assurance and security.
Part Tunneling:

You can pick which applications or sites utilize the VPN association and which utilize your customary web association assuming your VPN client upholds split burrowing.
End
Planning the VPN client is a significant push toward ensure that your VPN is specially crafted to your specific necessities. Marking in, picking a reasonable server region, and changing additional settings update the security and

execution of your VPN affiliation. For a consistent VPN experience, we will examine the useful aspects of connecting to the VPN, testing your connection, and identifying typical issues in the following sections of this guide.

6. Partner with the VPN

With the VPN client planned, connecting with the VPN is an unmistakable cycle. This step ensures that your web traffic is encoded and controlled through the picked server, giving you a protected and private web based knowledge.

6.1 Shipping off the VPN Client

Open the VPN Application:

On your gadget, begin the VPN client. This ought to regularly be conceivable from your workspace, structure plate, or wireless home screen.

Login (While perhaps Not At this point):

If you're not at present endorsed in, enter your username and secret expression to get to your VPN account.

6.2 Associate button for signing in:

Look for a "Point of interaction" or "Go" button inside the VPN client interface.

If the server is not selected, select one:

If you haven't picked a server as of now, the client could incite you to pick one going before partner. Follow the prompts to select a server location.

Connect:

Snap or tap the "Connection point" button to spread out a relationship with the VPN server.
Affiliation Status:

The VPN client will show the affiliation status. A powerful affiliation is typically shown by a green or related image.

6.3 Withdrawing from the VPN

Right when you're finished using the VPN, it's imperative for isolate to proceed with normal web access. Follow this technique:

Button for Disengage:

Within the VPN client interface, look for a button that says "Distinction" or "Stop."
Confirmation:

Reiterate that you must withdraw whenever provoked.
Affiliation Status:

The VPN client ought to indicate, frequently with a red or separated symbol, that you are not typically associated.
Note:
Modified Affiliation:

Some VPN clients offer an opportunities for modified affiliation when your device starts. If you think the VPN should communicate in this way, actually look at the settings.
Quick Interface:

The "Speedy Interface" option on some VPN clients directs you to the most recent or best server that anyone could hope to locate.

End

Partner with the VPN is a fundamental cycle that incorporates shipping off the VPN client, marking in, picking a server (if fundamental), and rocking the boat in and out of town button. Ensure that you withdraw when you're done to proceed with standard web access. In the following sections of this helper, we will cover testing your VPN affiliation, researching typical issues, and exploring advanced plans for a more revamped VPN experience.

7. Testing Your VPN Affiliation

Following partner with the VPN, it's basic to ensure that the affiliation is secure, private, and performing in a perfect world. Checking your IP address, really taking a look at the speed of your association, and searching for DNS spills are all essential for testing your VPN association.

7.1 Confirming Your IP Address

Go to a site that checks IP addresses:

The IP address showed should be the one given by your VPN, not your certified public IP address.
Region Check:

The site may similarly outfit information about the area related with the IP address. Promise it thinks about to the server region you picked.

7.2 Checking the Affiliation Speed

Use a Speed Test Site:

Run the Speed Test:

Start the speed test and keep a record of the results for both the transfer and download speeds.
With and without a VPN:

Contrast the speeds and the VPN related and isolated. While a slight lessening in speed is common, immense drops could exhibit issues.

7.3 DNS Hole Testing: Go to a DNS Break Testing Site:

Use a DNS spill testing site, for instance,

"https://www.dnsleaktest.com/" or "https://ipleak.net/".
Run the Test:

Run the test on the site and study the results. Make certain that the DNS servers that were recorded are associated with your VPN provider. Check for IPv6 Breaks:

A couple of locales in like manner check for IPv6 spills. Ensure that your IPv6 address isn't uncovered.
End
Testing your VPN affiliation is basic to ensure that it's functioning true to form. Checking your IP address, affirming affiliation speed, and testing for DNS spills are basic stages in assessing the security and execution of your VPN. In the going with region of this associate, we will explore researching typical

issues and look at advanced plans for those expecting to change their VPN experience further.

8. Investigating Normal Issues

Experiencing issues with your VPN association is entirely expected, yet with a precise methodology, numerous issues can be settled. Here are normal VPN issues and investigating moves toward assist you with tending to them:

8.1 Issue with Connections: Unfit to associate with the VPN server.

Investigating Steps:

Verify Your Internet Connection:

Guarantee that your web association is steady and working accurately.

Try a variety of servers:

Change to an alternate server inside the VPN client. Servers may occasionally experience problems or be temporarily unavailable.
Change VPN Conventions:

Explore different avenues regarding different VPN conventions (e.g., from OpenVPN to IKEv2). A few organizations or gadgets might require explicit conventions.
Firewall/Antivirus Obstruction:

Impair your firewall or antivirus briefly to check in the event that they are hindering the VPN association.

8.2 Sluggish Association Speed
Issue: Although a VPN connection has been established, internet speed is slow.

Investigating Steps:

Attempt Various Servers:

Interface with an alternate server to check whether the issue continues to happen. Server burden can influence speed.
Change VPN Conventions:

Explore different avenues regarding different VPN conventions. A few conventions might offer better execution relying upon your organization.
Check the bandwidth caps:

Confirm that there are no bandwidth restrictions on your VPN plan. Moving up to a higher-level arrangement might further develop speed.

Really take a look at Neighborhood Organization:

Guarantee that your neighborhood organization (Wi-Fi or Ethernet) isn't encountering issues. Restarting your switch might help. Problems with DNS or IP leaks: DNS or IP address data is releasing, compromising protection.

Investigating Steps:

Empower Off button:

On the off chance that your VPN client has an off button include, empower it to stop web traffic in the event that the VPN association drops.
Update VPN Client:

Guarantee that your VPN client is state-of-the-art. Designers frequently discharge updates to fix expected spills.

DNS Manual Configuration:

Physically arrange your gadget to utilize the DNS servers given by the VPN rather than the default ones.

Investigate IPv6 Leaks:

Incapacitate IPv6 on your gadget in the event that your VPN supplier doesn't uphold it to forestall IPv6 spills.

End

Investigating normal VPN issues requires a precise methodology, including really looking at web associations, exploring different avenues regarding various servers and conventions, and tending to possible holes. Consistently refreshing your VPN client and monitoring your VPN plan's restrictions can add to a smoother and safer experience. In the following segments, we will investigate progressed setups and best practices for utilizing a VPN successfully.

9. Utilizing the VPN Securely

Guaranteeing the protected and viable utilization of your VPN includes grasping different parts of its usefulness, conventions, and extra security highlights. To use your VPN safely, follow these guidelines and best practices:

9.1 Figuring out VPN Conventions

VPN conventions characterize the guidelines and cycles that oversee how information is sent between your gadget and the VPN server. Normal conventions include:

OpenVPN:

Generally viewed as secure and flexible. It's open-source, and numerous VPN suppliers support it.
IKEv2/IPsec:

Known for its speed and solidness. It is frequently used on portable devices.
L2TP/IPsec:

Gives solid encryption yet may not be just about as secure as different conventions. It's generally expected utilized when similarity is fundamentally important.
PPTP:

A more established convention that ought to be kept away from because of safety weaknesses.

9.2 Arranging Extra Security Elements

Off button:

In the settings of your VPN client, turn on the kill switch feature. This guarantees that assuming the VPN association drops suddenly, everything web traffic is stopped to forestall information spills.

Multifaceted Verification (MFA):

For an additional layer of security, enable multi-factor authentication if your VPN provider supports it. This regularly includes getting a code on your cell phone as well as entering your secret key.

Part Burrowing:

Some VPN clients offer split burrowing, permitting you to pick which applications or sites utilize the VPN association and which utilize your standard web association. Utilize this element carefully to adjust security and execution.

9.3 Refreshing the VPN Client

Stay up with the latest by routinely checking for reports on the supplier's site. Engineers discharge updates to address security weaknesses and work on in general execution.

In conclusion, using a VPN safely requires familiarity with its protocols, configuration of additional security features, and up-to-date client software. By following prescribed procedures, you can improve the security and protection of your internet based exercises. This guide's final sections will talk about disconnecting and reconnecting to the VPN, optional advanced configurations, and a summary of the advantages of using a VPN and best practices for using it.

10. Detaching and Reconnecting to the VPN

Appropriately dealing with your VPN association incorporates knowing how to detach and reconnect when vital. Whether you need to return to customary web access or address network issues, here's an aide on detaching and reconnecting to your VPN:

10.1 Removing Oneself from the VPN Launch the VPN Client:

On your device, start the VPN client. Find the Distinction Button:

Search for a "Distinction," "Stop," or comparative button inside the VPN client interface.
Snap or Tap to Detach:

Snap or tap the button to detach from the VPN server.

Affirm Detachment (whenever incited):

Some VPN clients might request affirmation prior to detaching. Affirm the activity whenever provoked.

Verify the Connectivity Status:

Guarantee that the VPN client shows a separated or inactive status.

10.2 Reconnecting to the VPN

Open the VPN Client:

On your device, start the VPN client. Login (While possibly Not As of now):

In the event that you're not currently signed in, enter your username and secret word to get to your VPN account.

Select Server (In the event that Not Picked):

In the event that you haven't chosen a server during the past meeting, the client could provoke you to pick one.

To connect, tap or click:

Within the VPN client interface, look for a button that says "Connect" or "Go."

Verify the Connectivity Status:

Guarantee that the VPN client shows an associated or dynamic status.

Note:

Automatic Linking:

Some VPN clients offer a possibility for programmed association when your gadget begins. Really look at the settings assuming you believe the VPN should interface naturally.
Fast Interface:

Some VPN clients have a "Speedy Interface" choice that naturally associates you to the last utilized or the most ideal that anyone could hope to find server.
Conclusion Managing your online privacy and security requires knowing how to disconnect and reconnect from your VPN. Whether you need to return to standard web access or address network issues, following these means guarantees a consistent progress. We will provide best practices for using a VPN effectively and a summary of

the advantages of using one in the final section of this guide.

11. High level Setups (Discretionary)

For clients looking for a more redone VPN experience or tending to explicit necessities, investigating progressed setups can be helpful. Here are discretionary designs that offer extra control and security:

11.1 Split Burrowing

Part burrowing permits you to conclude which applications or sites utilize the VPN association and which utilize your standard web association. This can be useful in advancing pace and overseeing assets.

Navigate to the VPN Client Settings:

Open the settings or inclinations menu of your VPN client.

Find Split Burrowing:

Search for a "Split Burrowing" or comparable choice.
Arrange Applications/Sites:

Pick explicit applications or enter site URLs to incorporate/reject from the VPN burrow.
Apply Changes:

Save your settings and apply the changes.

11.2 Off button Design

The off button is a basic security highlight that stops web traffic assuming the VPN association drops startlingly. Guarantee it is appropriately arranged for greatest adequacy.

Navigate to the VPN Client Settings:

Open the settings or inclinations menu of your VPN client.
Find Off button:

Empower Off button:

Empower the off button highlight.
Test Association:

Temporarily disconnect from the VPN to ensure that the kill switch works as intended.

11.3 Port Sending

Port sending can be helpful for specific applications or administrations that require explicit ports to be open. This is a high level element and may not be upheld by all VPN suppliers.

Check the VPN provider's support:

Check to see if your VPN service allows port forwarding.
Access VPN Client Settings:

Open the settings or inclinations menu of your VPN client.
Empower Port Sending:

Whenever upheld, search for a "Port Sending" or comparable choice and empower it.
Design Explicit Ports:

Enter the particular ports expected by the application or administration.
Apply Changes:

Save your settings and apply the changes.

11.4 Muddled Servers

Muddled servers are intended to sidestep web limitations and control in locales where VPN use is confined or checked.

Check the VPN provider's support:

Affirm assuming your VPN supplier offers jumbled servers.
Access VPN Client Settings:

Open the settings or inclinations menu of your VPN client.
Make Obfuscated Servers Available:

Whenever upheld, search for an "Jumbled Servers" or comparative choice and empower it.
Interface with Jumbled Servers:

Pick muddled servers while interfacing with the VPN.

End

High level designs give extra control and customization to clients with explicit necessities. However, not all VPN providers may support these features, and using them should be approached with awareness of the implications. We will provide best practices for using a VPN effectively and a summary of the advantages of using one in the final section of this guide.

12. All things considered, utilizing a Virtual Private Association

(VPN) is an effective method for updating on the web insurance, transparency, and security. This guide has strolled you through the whole course of making, arranging, and upgrading your VPN experience. Might we at some point recap the central issues and give several extra snippets of data:

Advantages of Utilizing a VPN:
Enhanced Safety:

VPNs scramble your web traffic, keeping untouchables away from looking at your online works.
Secure Information Transmission:

Your information is safeguarded from possible dangers as it voyages safely between your gadget and the VPN server.

Bypassing Geo-Cutoff points:

VPNs empower you to get to content that is limited by district by permitting you to associate with servers in different areas.

Secure Access from distant:

VPNs are basic for affiliations, giving areas of strength for a to representatives to get to affiliation assets from a good ways.

Anonymity:

By covering your IP address, virtual confidential organizations (VPNs) add an extra layer of namelessness to your internet based presence.

Best Practices for Utilizing a VPN:

Select a Reliable Expert association:

Choose a VPN provider based on its reputation, security features, and unquestionable dedication to client insurance.

Consistently Update the VPN Client:

Make sure you are up to date on the most recent security updates and components by staying informed.

Switch off the power:

If the VPN association out of nowhere quits working, continue to turn on the off button to forestall information spills.

Sort Programs:

Examine changed VPN shows and get the one that lines with your security and execution necessities.

Test Your Membership:

Intermittently test your VPN relationship with guarantee it is secure, private, and performing ideally.

Examine Optional Advanced Arrangements:

Research advanced features like split tunneling, port sending, jumbled servers, and something different for clients who need to change.

Separate When Not Required:

Separate from the VPN when you shouldn't worry about its confirmation to develop web speed and execution.

Keep revived:

Remain informed about restores, security rehearses, and any developments in the VPN scene.

You can profit from your VPN and have a safeguarded and classified electronic understanding by keeping these principles. Recollect that the possibility of a VPN besides relies on cautious and informed use. Remain watchful, remain secure!

www.ingramcontent.com/pod-product-compliance
Lightning Source LLC
Chambersburg PA
CBHW060210260726

48658CB00005BA/1963